Gold That Frames the Mirror

൫

poems by Brandon Melendez

Write Bloody Publishing

writebloody.com

First edition.
ISBN: 978-1938912870

Cover Design by Derrick C. Brown
Interior Layout by Winona León
Edited by David Perez, Gary Edwin Lovely, and Derrick C. Brown
Proofread by Keaton Maddox
Author Photo by Lindsey Michelle

Type set in Bergamo from www.theleagueofmoveabletype.com

Section break image: *Hummingbird* by Carl Holderness, licensed under CC BY.

Printed in the USA

Write Bloody Publishing
Los Angeles, CA

Support Independent Presses
writebloody.com

For My Parents,
Teresa & David Melendez

GOLD THAT FRAMES THE MIRROR

GOLD THAT FRAMES THE MIRROR

. . . cavo esta tierra para encontrar los ídolos
y hacerme una historia.
—Virgilio Piñera

It is not down in any map; true places never are.
—Herman Melville

SYNONYMS FOR BORDER

fringe |::| fraying boundary |::| line separating two political or geographical areas, especially countries |::| countries that flood in & out of each other's gaping bodies |::| body of water that does not end with the horizon |::| edge of the map & the ghost ships anchored there |::| gold that frames the mirror |::| petroleum coating the tongue with coins |::| limit of geography unmarked by bloody hands |::| asymptote of eyes refusing to close |::| end of an executive order & the dead that come after |::| flank |::| surrounded by steel |::| curve of a corral & the horse's broken jaw |::| distance two people cross to say I love you |::| the emptying of language & the bodies that unspool in its wake

In a City Old as Smallpox in a Peroxide White Room, My Therapist Asks a Question about Coping

Somewhere in Oakland,
a warehouse catches fire

& the people I love trapped
inside inhale enough monoxide

to smother the whole sleeping city. Elsewhere,
a friend overdoses & I add his name

to the list of ancestors made holy
by a needle shoveled through skin.

Before Christendom, *holy* meant preserved
whole & indivisible. A stone pillar

that cannot be unstoned. Across the Atlantic,
someone I spent a summer with

playing chess on a south Berkeley rooftop
is carried off a plane past rows of weeping

mothers, his heart stopped midair.
What does it mean to leave this world

from one country but never arrive
elsewhere, to become an entry

in someone's catalogue of empty seats.
An hour ago, an hour outside of Boston

a boy was sitting in his driveway
when a nearby chimney collapsed

like a ransacked church, burying him.
I can't stop wondering who

he was waiting for. Was it his mother?
An old friend? How many of us wasted today

waiting for a familiar face
& instead, instead . . .

DESMADRE

Grandmother describes my Spanish as desmadre. She means my accent

    is the wreckage after the storm. Proof our family washed up

in this country one day   & were no longer from anywhere else.

    Desmadre, directly translated, means *without mother*.

Grandmother's history is a map I lost & have been searching for

    ever since.   I have a theory: the voyage will end

with my mouth open   the last relic of la patria

    settling on my tongue for a moment before dissolving

into the water. Or, another theory: I am not the wreckage

    but the storm—the unexpected wave that drowns the woman

bringing her family home. The sandy brine that breaks through

    the hull   & ruins all her books.

ARCHITECTURE OF REFUGE

My first memory is an open gate.
On the other side my father sits
in our living room, molding a castle
from clay. Each steeple & drum tower:
a brother, a son reaching out in praise
or prayer. My father laughs as my small

& feckless hands carve through his kingdom
like a scythe. He laughs knowing he can build
something new from the rubble. Stronghold.
Hideout. Call it *resurrection*. Call it making room
for joy; a boy learning the architecture of refuge

from his father. A boy unaware of all the ways
the earth demands breath as payment for breath.
Ask me now of my father's heart attack; I'll speak
only of the room we all gathered in.
There were so many lights, none of us had a shadow.
I hugged my father & learned

how quick someone's arms become a house
you can die in. & *father* is not a synonym
for immortal. Or maybe it is. After all, today
his heartbeat still has music inside—refuses
to end its simple meter. I want to believe
this is what love does: it keeps the body going

after the heart gives out. Once, I opened
my wrist like a book of prayers & all the lights
in the house broke into a thin stream of glass.
I found myself in a room, empty
except for my father's clay-stained hands. I reached
towards them—leaving behind a trail of bayonets.

I kept reaching but never quite got a hold.
Ask me now why I did it & I'll say
I never meant to.
I never meant to be the reason why
my father stopped laughing.

That Time I Went North & Woke Up with a New Face

the last person i truly loved[1] married someone with my name

not me of course   i am too full of cities to lay on a single bed

of grass   eventually every blade will be concrete

pulled across my skin   i imagine the other man snatched this name

of mine   like an urn from a burning house[2]   & he threw the ash

inside across the los angeles basin   there it grew into a field

of daffodils & diamonds   & who wouldn't dream to shine like that?

to have a bouquet of faces someone will love until one of you dies

or until you are no longer bright enough to call morning

i'm not sure how the story is supposed to end[3]   was i the one who

torched the house?   who took scissors to the carpet

& snapped the gas pipes behind the stove   wasn't i the one

who pointed to the edge of a map   & then flew across it?[4]

i don't mean to harvest old bruises like overripe plums

but today someone said my name   & it no longer belonged to me

---

1 when i say *truly loved* i mean my car was towed outside your house once & sometimes i still wake up stranded in north hollywood

2 somewhere near the intersection of camarillo & lankershim

3 i can't recall exactly but my hands are now a freeway if you look close enough you can see us driving across california if you look closer the car is empty & the freeway is empty & these are just hands & not the distance between us

4 i imagine it now like you rolled over in bed one morning & then

& rather than face the ways I've become absence[5]

i throw smooth stones off a bridge in berkeley

resent the way the river ripples   salivating for more   the adage

about water[6] & the mirror is a dirty lie   nothing i see below

looks anything like me   though i can't stop staring at the minnow

floating belly-up by the rocks   its scales still glistening in the light

& what a strange thing   to have a face that glitters   even after

---

5

6 remember how we were water how the dolphins wet the back of our throats & we
spilled out from the river? remember how we flooded the car from the inside a torrent
of rebellious tongue remember how no one can touch the same river twice remember
how we never touched again

DRY/SPELL

Es diciembre, y nuestros huesos aún raspan

contra el suelo reseco. Abuela se sienta

en el jardín de atrás y protege San Diego.

Ella bebe de su vaso y comienza a llover.

Besa a mi padre en su frente

y la sequía se acaba. Hace que la magia

parezca su primer idioma. Mira

cómo ella hace que el desierto llore.

Mira cómo ella conjura este hechizo

de agua y sal. Ella lo llama por su nombre,

lo llama: tierra no conquistada. Un gallo cercano

comienza a cantar y no cede. Cada gota de lluvia

es un nuevo día.

PORTRAIT OF GRIEF AS A MANICURED LAWN

grass is both a bed

                     & a blade

either you rush in

              scraping your shins

against the jagged jade stocks

            or you lie barefoot

among the weeds counting ants

 as they parade past dressed

        in black

                 regardless

you must find a way across

before you make

your exit.

Shouts to Scene Kids

& the early days of Myspace, pic4pic
& perfect-angled photos, eyeliner
we applied on the morning bus

with no mirror. buccaneers
of the black band tee, black
nail polish, black hair bleached & dyed

back. shouts to Hot Topic, sanctuary
of all things goth & ghost. home

to every goat-headed boy in a goat-
headed costume. Jack Skellington sang

This Is Halloween & October didn't end.
instead we dressed drop-dead gorgeous

all year. ripped our fishnet gloves & gauged
our ears, laced our shoes for the show. shouts
to every garage turned punk rock turned

mosh pit, spin kick, windmill, spit lobbed
in the air like arrows of flint. We kids
of tusk & antler, animals of strange

rage & a particular brand of sadness.
shouts to sadness as a fucking brand.

a badge, a band where every member
is someone you hope makes it through
high school. first period junior year

I remember Alex saying she wanted to die
& I laughed & she laughed

but she left lunch in an ambulance
with sixty pills thawing in her stomach.

for four days no one played a single song.
when she finally came back to school

she wore her favorite black jacket

the one with a patch of a girl pulling
herself out of a pond by her own hair.

I didn't know what to ask so I asked,
are you okay & she said, *yeah.*
she said, *I outlived who I was yesterday.*

like if you live long enough to forgive
yourself you've won the game. & shouts
to that. shouts to survival—a mirror

that looks the most gorgeous
clad in black.

Etymology of Absence, Ending in My Grandmother Singing "México en la Piel"

Spanish is a language of blood. Armada that unleashed

land-starved men on sleeping villages & raised an empire

from the husk of gutted flesh. But blood also reads as family.

Family as Mexico. Mexico as a ravine teeming with old corridos

& the rivers rimmed with yucca. This lineage does not belong

to me & also does. Spanish is the first love song

my grandmother learned, the last bridge

between her voice & the emptying field of my American accent.

It is the timbre of her laugh as she shouts ¡ay que lindo!

& presses her lips to my cheek. She pauses

like she came a very long way to give me this desert

wet with promise. Her hands still swollen

pomegranates from an unforgiving sun. Spanish, the sound of bare feet

hammering a path in sand. The sound my family silenced

to hand me this new country, a mouth unburdened by mariachi.

But can I understand this sacrifice if I cannot pronounce it?

O grandmother's voice. Song of silt rising from the throat.

Each callus & raw gumline a melody of la fuerza

that has not been gagged with a ruby pommel. It's true,

I want my tongue to move like hers. To have words roll

out of my mouth, an avalanche of machete & molasses.

But my grandmother's tongue is not a commodity I can barter

for a history that does not end in borders. Heritage is more

than mastering language. More than pulling out walls

from between teeth. Heritage is a refusal to erase or be erased.

A refusal to bury traditional song in an unmarked grave or dub

a grandmother's love in English. If nothing else, today I hear

her rejoice into a chorus of ¡Así se siente México,

Así se siente México! & I understand: when people say the tongue

is the strongest muscle in the body, they mean it is strong enough

to hold an entire history on its back & still sing.

LINE/AGE

if you trace my grandparents back to the fire   they stepped out from

you will find a room   with beheaded gods   floating in jars of vinegar

a horse with two broken legs   guarding an adobe church

if you go back further   you will find a knife   tucked inside

a blank map   a single bronze coin   levitating on the horizon

is it so hard to imagine   my grandparents come from more

than a trail of open graves   even if they don't have the paper

to prove it   even if they can't stand ankle deep in the Rio Grande

without being washed away

I discover the severed head of a jaguar   sitting in a dry riverbed

& ask my grandfather what it means   he says follow the blood

back to its body   trace the red dirt with your finger   you'll find

what you're looking for   you'll find someone else   got there first

ORIGIN :: PREDISPOSITION

I was born & immediately evacuated from the hospital.

Before my mother could hold me, gloved men

severed the umbilical cord & dragged me out

of town. Though it was for my own good.

I needed a bigger hospital, better doctors.

I came into this world with a hole in my lung;

slugtunnel & perforated flesh. My first urge

was to wail—then to grab the doctor's stethoscope,

scissors, latex & press them into my chest.

A first desperate attempt to clot what strange

emptiness lived in me. Before object permanence,

before hunger, I knew something inside me

could not be filled. Another boy perhaps,

with a face not quite mine, sitting below my sternum

eating grass, ash, his own hands. The doctors will tell you

the years have stitched his mouth into regular meat,

the hole sealed over. But I know the boy survived,

he just learned to hide his appetite for metal

& metastasis. He begs softly & only after the room

goes dark. Yes, to be sure if you cut me open

you would discover I look exactly

like all the men in my family.

Los Fantasmas, or If You've Seen Coco You'll Understand Why I Didn't Stop Crying for a Week After

Grandmother believes in los fantasmas. She says these spirits dance

free from their skeletons & into the wind. They cackle & howl

as they look over us from street lights & old books. She says

los fantasmas have strange ways of telling us things. Grandfather died

on his birthday, on the eightieth anniversary of his becoming

flesh. A wailing storm of limbs—he left his body like an exhale

or a hymn that heaves into the sky. My uncle says my grandfather

would have interrupted his own the funeral procession if he could.

He mutinied against anything that cut the music off—or made the body

go limp. Shortly before he died, my grandfather said, *at my wake,*

bring me a mariachi band. Tell them to play "When the Saints Go Marching In"

& expect me to come marching in. Los fantasmas have a strange way

of making us listen. I knew my grandfather was gone for good when I woke

with a song lodged in my head & I had no way to write it down.

Glass Pulled from the Wreckage Like a Body Still Breathing

O heaven forged of mirrors
    but reflecting no one's dead
        face   vacuum of stars
    that never supernovas

instead pearls into the pupils
    of the child I once was
        who thought miracles
    had my mother's voice

    that is until
    the accident

until the car collapsed
    in on itself
        taking all light with it

I still don't know how she made it out

whether she crawled
    from between mangled
        metal or pushed through
    the glass like a ghost returning
        to the world

the doctors let me visit
    & through the window
        I saw her
    still heaving with life

I bolted towards her

remember:
    if you hold someone
        at just the right angle
in front of two mirrors

    they go on forever

The Author Becomes a Moirologist

You handed me a box of moth-orchids you let die,
the ones I bought for our bedroom. & I said thank you
like you had given me money to buy a new shirt—

which is how I knew we no longer loved each other.
Both of us—just waiting for an excuse to leave.
For weeks after, the California countryside burned

out the window & on the evening news & the ash
growing in my cheeks became the only way
to pronounce home. So I left.

I spat cinders out the car window on I-80 east
until I could no longer see smoke. I drove & drove
past fence & oil spill, cattle farm & slaughterhouse.

I saw a farmer carry a goat down a hill in Nebraska.
A woman ran across the freeway in Illinois
to escape a thunderstorm. I counted a total of thirteen

dead dogs spread along the median. I imagined
adopting them. Exactly as they are. Rubber-singed
& rotten with flies. Or at least giving them a proper burial.

Don't we all deserve cleaner, happier exits?
Someone who will cry at the funeral? If you're rich enough,
you can hire someone to bawl into a black veil, to fling

their shivering body onto your casket. Some people
make a living this way. I bet with practice
I could make a great professional mourner. Bring me

your plants, pets, relatives—anything you can't let go.
I'll say thank you, thank you so much. I'll grab a rag
soaked with oil & tallow, & fall to my knees, devastated.

IN THE STORY, THE ROLE OF AHAB IS PLAYED BY MY FATHER

Somewhere in the Atlantic, Ahab hunts

down the whitest monster in the ocean,

harpoon in one hand, lantern in the other.

It is not new moon madness that makes him boil

with bloodlust, but rather what was stolen.

Vendetta of lost skin & sinew—femur fermenting

inside the whale's belly. Instead of wood,

Ahab asked the carpenter to craft his new leg

with whalebone. He knew in order to protect himself

from what wants to kill him, he must become it.

In Defense of Hella

Praise this relic of an endless California
    summer housed in my throat.
How it spills over like a fist

full of gold coins & refuses to apologize
    for its excess. When I say hella
I mean I dipped my feet

in the San Francisco Bay
    & watched a mountain
of doubloons rise up

& glitter around my waist. Hella
    is how I measure Telegraph
Avenue from Fox Theater

to the empty lot on Haste—
    the one with the word stolen
graffitied over a sunset.

Hella redwoods outlived

    Columbus & Cortés

& hella people buried beneath

the roots did not. Hella

    is the count of ancestors

who blossom across California

& Mexico & how many cities

    have been built

from their bones. Hella is each

new brick & cobblestone street

    I am not native to

but still call home. I know it's better

I left for Boston, for somewhere

    that snows. Here—I can walk

through a cemetery & only notice

the flowers. I am tired of mourning

    ancient thievery & there is enough

displacement happening

without me collecting avenues

    to fill my pockets.

When I say hella I mean here

are all the people I carry with me

    made of gold.

The First Time I See My Father Cry He Is Pulling Me from the Water to Unsing Alcoholism

son, not all gods die
    with their disciples

some swim inside the artery.

I cannot count all the holes
    in our lineage

made by this god's hunger.

god that turns men into meat
    into myth.

god of thirst. of serrated
    tooth & sea turtles

gored by ragged hooks.
    god who commands

the ocean floor to swell
    inside you.

god of god-
    less reef, insatiable

in his lust for pilgrimage.

pillar of sacrament
    & cirrhosis bottle-

necked through
    a gagging throat.

  god of your grandfather,

of gutterwater & gold.
　　god who lives

in the aperture between
　　your body

& its wreckage.
　　god of ships.

god of sailors caught
　　in the rage

of a ram-headed sea.
　　god of desperation

who makes saltwater
　　shimmer & taste

of honeysmoke, who serenades
　　you songs of salvation

while your mouth fills
　　with salt.

song of rapture.

song of drowning. psalm

that holds dying men
　　in its belly, all of them

wearing your face.

As Respite from Insomnia, the Author Writes an Elegy for What the Night Took

None of the streetlights in my neighborhood work.
Night passes through each avenue unimpeded,
gorging its cheeks with asphalt & rubber & telephone wires.
A bird, mistaking the single bulb of my room for refuge,
flies full tilt into the double pane window
& snaps against the glass. I am helpless to stop the breakage.
All I can do is collect the blue-gray feathers
trapped in my screen & set them on the bookshelf.
I curse Edison & Tesla & my herringbone buttons,
condemn myself to a lifetime of carrying soft things
I am unable to save. Outside, the unsettled silence is invaded
by a medley of nearby songbirds. Their tune, a tomb of light
sharp as a scythe. Do they not hear their chorus ring
a bit softer than the night before? I do not understand.
What good is joy if you cannot mourn what is lost
in the name of light?

ALPRAZOLAM

My chest, a jar
of honey—knifed
open. I know sweet
is the most sweet
while it gags you,
makes you ask
to be sacrificed.
I'd forfeit an organ
for silence. Suture
my ears to stop
the angry hum
of wings inside me.
Hand me a blade, bees-
wax & I'll show you
what I'm made of.
Did you know anyone
can be a graveyard
if you dig deep enough?
Did you know at the edge
of every scalpel
there is a prayer? Imagine
this simple vivisection:
I make an incision
from chin to sternum.
I drop a small white
pearl down my throat
& like a song
a hive of humming bees
flies out.

Conjuring

I am my father's son sure

    but not my father's sun-blistered skin

so why do I keep conjuring this genealogy

    of limbs like each skeleton belongs to me

let's say this bloodline is a border I walk on

    but never across & home is whatever earth

my father's hands have watered let's say

    I come from people who carved clavicle

& vertebrae into a staircase

    who told me to climb

        & never look back

ETHOS OF   I   C   E

erasure of the Immigration & Customs Enforcement mission statement

We   the nation's
           criminal   border
security   threaten   public safety and exploit
America's   l and

We   the   sophisticated   g   u   n

We   the   rage   and
               grit
stand

          for   cell   s

We use   force
       to   form

         a   border   in   our
communities and we keep   the streets

LUPUS

my mother's veins are kennels
filled with feral dogs.

in each of their mouths, a hand
that once fed them, & now
feeds them its own frayed nerves.

feverwild, the dogs mistake
their legs for prey. pitter
pat of rabbit paw or fox
between burrows.

when a body hunts its own reflection,
it's a miracle there's anything left
but pelt.

but you should see my mother,
hounds & all, she walks unshod
right out into the forest carrying

lavender & coltsfoot & the hunters
hush fearing the muzzle.

I WATCH THE FAMILY MOVE INTO THE HOUSE AT THE END OF THE BLOCK

& remember how a man hung himself in that garage
on the hottest day of July & his daughter walked in

to discover his body a little closer to god. Rumor was she found
the family dog nuzzled beneath her father's legs but it flashed

its yellow teeth, growling whenever she got too close.
For a week the news boiled the air in our neighborhood.

Anyone who drove past that house said they could feel
their throat start to char, skin unravelling like rope. One woman swore

her terrier gnawed through his leash & leaped into traffic
just to avoid the house. Of course, by Sunday everyone was back

mowing their lawns & drinking Coors out on the fresh paved asphalt.
All the teenagers gathered at the community pool to drink vodka

& escape ourselves, to count the years until we leave this city
without season, this forever empty sky. As far as I know

no one saw the man's daughter after that. She barricaded

the front door with plywood one evening & was gone.

No one knows if she ever came back for the dog.

But months passed & the summer heat stayed muzzled inside

the house all year. I know this because when the U-Haul

pulled into the driveway this morning & the garage door

creaked open for the first time since, two rows of gnarled teeth

lurched out & disappeared into the open air.

AMERICAN BOY SHARES DEATH METAL WITH HIS ABUELO
after "Turn Loose the Doves" *by It Dies Today*

what did you call this again, mijo?

dead metal?   metal devil? can you turn it up?

can you turn it into the sound of something

other than la caballeria set loose on children

crossing a river?   ¡híjole!   there is a butcher

trapped in the drum beat   or is it men

tearing into each other?   or the thump of doves

shot dead?   this sounds more like mutiny

than music   maybe the sorrow & misery are honest

but what of all the ways a song can heal?   it's a marvel

how often rage ruins the moment   how a man can stand

at the mouth of a lake & still burn

men spend their whole lives furious at others

for the mistakes we make. we don't know flight

like we know fight   & it's always ugly, mijo   how can you sit

with the violence done to a body & call it melody?

there is enough fractured in the world without a drum

thrashing like crushed mariposa wings   so tell me

how can you call this music? there's no grito!

no *ra-cha-cha* that makes you turn your body

into a cathedral   makes you worthy

of worship the way your lungs come loose

mijo, what good is music if two people can't dance

their last first dance to it? the truth is—every day

since I met your grandmother has been a song

chorus of crimson doves   I'm not saying it's been perfect

I'm saying I know it's love because I hear maracas

& become young again   at home in the hands I want to bury me

listen   I cannot hear the word *metal*   & not think *weapon*

I want to explain what anger does to men like us

perhaps one day I'll tell the story   for now I'll say

if there is violence in this family   it dies with me

no mourning   no funeral   a quiet exit   & I hope

the next time you hear a chorus that reminds you

of all you've survived   you'll start to understand

how good music ferries you into a future

where heaven is so close   there is no choice but to sing

PORTRAIT OF ANXIETY AS LIMINAL SPACE

a car circles through a roundabout

                                    searching for an exit

when a deer

      gallops through the windshield

                          & then another & another

& the barrage doesn't stop

                  the car rages forward as the road swells

with fresh fur coats

      the coats come back to life as deer

                      just in time to be impaled

by the incoming car

                        & for the life of me

i can't tell if i'm driving

                    or if i'm even in the car

          i might just be standing there

                            waiting

Raw, or My Therapist Asks Me to Describe the Feeling without Using "I" Statements

today sadness is not loud

no drunk orchestra of horns

braying inside a beat mule

no beat no mutiny

today sadness is soft

& small   a plucked crow

vibrating in a tub of milk

muffled yip   & limbs

that don't swing

as much as spread

like wings of singed meat

today sadness mistakes

the drain for an exit

opens its mouth to scream

& white rushes   in

Every Time I See My Ex, Shit Gets Kafkaesque

& there you are
on the opposite end
of the bus, eating
a blood orange. Overripe
& acerbic, the juice spills
onto the seat beside you.
You spot me & drop
the rotting fruit
into the soft
denim of your lap;
your mouth still
sticky with pulp.
The bus doors swing
open & as each person
files onboard
they burst
into a haze of horseflies
that rush straight
for your gums, still red
with feast. you vanish
beneath the fog
of famished wings
until the flies drop
dead: cooked by their own greed.
you stay gone & the only evidence
you were ever here
is a single rind;
a cluster of eggs
caught in my throat.

Reino, or I See My Grandfather by the Side of the Road, about Where He's Buried, but He's Wandering around with a Flag of Vertebrae

He is dead though.
    Doesn't this make him American

enough to demand the land
    he was buried in as his?

Doesn't this entitle him to break
    bread with gods

whose names fill the sky
    with anvils?

Or was he buried in random,
    easily forgotten earth?

Because I saw a truck
    drive over his grave

like that isn't how people
    get cursed, like that driver

isn't going to crack open
    their jaw tomorrow & spill out

ratones, conejos, cucarachas,
    & all their teeth.

    |::|

Who's to say this soil
    is American anyway,

like have you asked
    my grandmother?

She once swore
    the whole of California

belongs to her mother
    & my father still

calls this dead man
    Reino. That's right, the whole

damn kingdom. Grandfather was,
    after all, an unruly man

he once pulled his spine
    out of a screaming mouth

& carried that hurt
    until the end.

Who's going to tell him
    he can't still reign

from the dirt?

    | :: |

    The US government

denied my grandfather
    a military funeral,

denied they ever held him
    against a gun

& called them both
    by the same name.

The official reason they gave
    was my grandfather

did not join the Marines
    legally. Fine.

But he still volunteered
        to walk into any slaughter-

house with a crown
        of bullets in each hand.

They could have
        at least sent a flag,

or the address
        of that truck driver,

or a throne.

TAPHEPHOBIA, THE MORNING AFTER I LEARN CHESTER BENNINGTON TOOK HIS OWN LIFE

In the 18th century cholera flooded Europe
& all the faucets

in people's bodies opened. They leaked
& leaked until the coma set in. This yawning

sleep was so often mistaken for quietus
that the fear of live burial

bloomed like bacterium. Mania wet
& septic. To prevent more

accidental entombment,
a German doctor mechanized a coffin

with bells the dead could rattle
if they awoke gasping,

lungs filled with muddy oxygen
& an urge towards resurrection.

    |::|

The human body can lose a fifth
of its water before the coma sets in.

Before sleep is a box nailed shut. Afterward
we exist only in endings, in dirge

& dirt. I've been to enough funerals
to know that at the heart

of every cathedral there is an organ
gasping for air. The tune pushes

through a depressed cavity into a sick,
sick sadness. I've learned what I can

& cannot handle. What body I have left
when I am no longer water.

I can lose a fifth of myself
before depression sets in,

before all the songs in my head go silent
& after, I can only talk about myself

as ending. My throat, a carillon tower
flooding with the musician still inside.

    | :: |

I've learned depression
is the name we give to gravity

when we demand a diagnosis.
It is both the casket & the cavity waiting

with its eager mouth.
I am afraid that someday

I will catch myself sleeping
& reach for a spade. This morning

before I could open my eyes
I pushed my ear toward my chest

& waited
hoping to hear bells.

BLOOD PAGEANTRY

The man sitting next to me at Porter Square
    station wears his fur coat

like he named the animal after his father
    & then skinned the hide himself. He watches me

read a book where the author says too much
    about the body, about the origin of pilgrimage

 & plunder. The man turns to me & says, *you ever notice*
    how all poems are either about love or death?

He says this like no one has ever thought to name
    this blood pageantry for the spectacle that it is,

like we don't parade the people we've buried
    & unburied on purpose. I know what I'm doing

when I say today all my old lovers wake
    with a mouth full of soil, bed of soil; sky, soil.

No one gets a name. Instead: carnations, basic grief, elegy
    that can be read at the local theater. My ancestors, alive

as if for the first time, rise to greet each other, kiss
    while staring down barrels of agave

& muskets, write wedding vows, watch their countries
    empty from plague or famine or men

convinced if they name something in a new language
    the old one dies.

SERPENT CROWN LINED WITH MARROW

The Aztecs had eight omens that foretold
the arrival of the conquistadors
& almost all of them ended in fire.
Orange plume against the moon,
a burning temple & the storm of light
that cleaved the sky. Lake Texcoco
boiled up & seared Tenochtitlan down
to the bone. Eventually, a mirror appeared
on an ashen crane. Eventually, war horses
descended from salt & brought with them
a god with skin of abscess. What is the end
if not a new fire? If not the spectacle of silver
unsheathed for the first time? If not hands that
reach out in awe before vanishing?

    | :: |

I reach out in awe before vanishing
into my father's shoulder. My father vanishes
into a single tremor. I've never seen him break
like that: a wave pounding its head against
hospital doors, demanding they spit his father
back out & the man be brought back unmarked
by grief, grayslick & glossed with bloom.
This country tested my grandfather with a knife
of marrow, a bottle, an endless unlit street,
& finally won. I spent so many years listening
to his stories before understanding them as history
that must survive us. It's too late for him
to hear me, I know. But I haven't stopped trying,
I've only started to name my grandfather.

|::|

I only started to name my grandfather *abuelo*
after he died, Jesús instead of Jess after
he could no longer correct my Spanish.
This is poor magic for resurrection. I cannot
chant *Jesús, Jesús* as incantation & expect
abuelo to rise three days later. I can practice
his name until it no longer sounds like an apology.
But it will still be an apology. Music playing
into an empty room. The room fills with guitarróns,
then fades. Escucha, escucha: somewhere,
the distant thrum of ranchera & a bald man laughs,
swings his brittle hip, & curses his joints
for their bad memory. A boy refuses to dance
& he ages; cursing his perfect memory.

    | :: |

Cursing his perfect memory for its decay,
my father says childhood is a starved fog.
Labyrinth of locked doors, if only he saved
the keys. If only he kept a better atlas. He once
travelled this country to archive its scroll
& scripture, to carve a space for us. He's never
stopped, really. So how far must he go before
it's considered exodus? How many people
must know the story before it's canon? It's strange
irony; a historian glutted with so many centuries
that decades start leaving him in the night.
A good son, I memorize his hands, careful
joy, arroyo between resilient teeth, but I am
a reckless historian, I get ink on all the bones.

|::|

A reckless historian, I get ink on all the bones,
rewrite their stillness as reliquary, mistake
headstone for gemstone. Forgive me. If my hands
stop moving they will forget where they learned
this choreography; how they reach down time's
infinite throat & find a spine, a snake. Salvage
its tongue. Forgive me. I was born to my father
already mid-story & I haven't stopped listening.
As he tells it, there is empire before empire,
history before historia. It starts with a skull
in a jaguar's unflinching jaw. Crack of stone
against the mountain. Moctezuma climbs the temple
steps, burns copal. Quetzalcoatl appears at the tree
line. Then, thunder, the smell of gunpowder.

|::|

                    the storm of

        salt
                                    end
                                    of silver
                                    hands

I   vanish
                    My father vanishes

    marked by grief

        country

                                    listen
to   history
            survive us

                    name my grandfather.

                                    abuelo

This   magic for resurrection
chant *Jesús*   expect
abuelo to rise   practice
                                    apology

into an empty room

Escucha

        ranchera   laughs

        A
        perfect memory

          for us

     the story
        glutted with

joy   resilient

rewrite
headstone for gemstone

        I was born
   mid-

          crack of

    thunder
  | :: |

THEOREM WITH STAIRCASE & HUMMINGBIRD

The adage goes: age is not measured
in years but in baggage. Another fall
gone & I drag my body up the stairs.
The stairs line with people I love

who will not last the winter.
I want to believe if I don't
reach the end no one dies.

But I know that's not
how this works. My pockets
will keep filling with wax
& names. Cement & names.

& it will always be too late
to ask questions. I text a dead
number, anyway. Ask it to split
another round of drinks. No one

answers. I say: I'd settle for tea,
we could sit by the hearth & wrap
ourselves in all the sweaters
lovers have left behind.

Still, no answer. I say fine.
I don't delete the number.
Instead, I empty myself
of mezcal & mint.

I don't know which is heavier:
goodbye or the silence that smothers it.
Please, no more stairs. No more winters.
Let me sit in peace beneath sunlight.

Leave the window open
& let the hummingbirds land
on the sill before they fly

out of frame. Let me tell them
the vanishing point is a lie.
Anyone who leaves

for one horizon or another
curves away & towards you
all at once.

I Feel Most Like Myself with Painted Nails

Rouge sunset battered
atop each finger

a small galaxy
of comet & solar flare,

I am a god
of these two hands

& today let there be
unapologetic light.

Let there be an origin
story that is not bruised

fruit lodged in the throat
like a knife with no hilt.

When someone says
man the fuck up, they mean

what breathing thing
have you made

into a wound? What wounds
have you worn as trophy?

I try to name
a masculinity

that is not a wolf
masked in the body

of a wolf
& I end up howling

at the white fist pressed
into the night's soft cheek.

I'm sorry I'm not
sorry I undressed

myself of knuckles today.
I imagined a universe

not dipped in blood
 & made myself drip

with starlight.
I walked out

the front door
& marveled

at the way everything I touch
shines.

Field Notes on Desire

If scientists are to be believed, then touch has always been a lie.
Don't look at me. Blame our molecules

for the ways we are caged to our electrical orbits.
Every rushed kiss & brushed cheek are a trick

of the imagination, our brains trying to understand the world
as closer than it is. The truth is a lonely electromagnetism.

The universe propelling away from itself into an unknown
absence. So when I lie in bed, alone or otherwise, I am not

in bed really, but levitating above the voltage
of my own body. I touch nothing. But I am expected to try

to find myself in the maw of another, so fine. Let's say
I'm not alone. Let's say I've invited someone

over because I love nothing if not the lie. The hope
that maybe this time my want will take a shape

other than wine poured down a bleach white sink.
Defiant spillage. Brief but unrelenting vacancy. Like anyone

I can mistake heat for intimacy. I can mistake intimacy
for not wanting to die alone. But if I'm being honest

it still feels like a lie.

|::|

Here is something for us
to hold onto. Something true
to carry to the end
of the story: I have a body
until someone decides they deserve it
more.

|::|

Forgive me

    I don't mean

to take up

      so much space

    discussing

all the ways

    I am

absent

  | :: |

Maybe, I am wrong to hypothesize
about this machine. Maybe, the truth is as simple
as I feel broken. Rotten with rust & pink moss.
An emptied furnace in place of each organ
& everywhere in me coal & copper wire
& an engineer's severed arm trapped inside
bent gears.

Look. What I am trying to say is this: often, I wonder
why I am incapable of performing the most basic function
of a body. Take hunger. Someone says, *open* & a dam breaks,
a gated neighborhood is set on fire. Someone asks,
what do you want? & I show them a perfectly set dinner table,
a lake with a single floating lantern among the lilies.

I say, *don't touch*.
I say, *like anyone I want nothing more than to feel
desired*.

I want to desire like the rest, to crawl through the dark
or into bed & be happy with whatever hand finds me,
because hands are good enough.

But when it comes time. When I'm supposed to prove
this flesh is worth the price
of teeth, I unbutton my shirt & reveal nothing but thin wire
& a path through me.

Maybe I am not broken,
Maybe, I need someone who understands
when I say *machine*, I mean be *patient with me*.

|::|

Don't be surprised
if you go to touch me
& I've already left
out the back window.
I have this theory
that someone snuck in one night
& replaced my eyes
with fire escapes.
That must be why
I understand the world best
as an exit.

| :: |

ETYMOLOGY OF ABSENCE, ENDING IN A STILL LIFE OF THE RIO GRANDE AT SUNSET

Hernán Cortés said, *let there be light* & the temple of Huitzilopochtli
burst into flame. He said, *let there be a river of gold* & its shimmer was
ripped from the skin of antique gods. Spanish spread like a plague of
hooves, like water stampeding up a mountain.

& there's the story of the vultures that sit swollen-
bellied by the marsh. The people who had their tongues cut
& fed to mosquitoes.

This is not genesis but perhaps, the origin of running.
Who was the first person in my lineage to outrun a warship,
a spear, a soldier? Who was the first to wield language like a sword?
All I know is my family fled north

until they no longer recognized the sound of their own footsteps.
Spanish is the smoke lining the trail. The truck revving
through sand & tar. Spanish is the house they built

out of gravestones. A grayrot alchemy. Of course, my foremothers
did not wish their children's children to mourn the meadow
our teeth grew from. Instead, I was taught English like a bullet
to keep wet between my gums. Something to flash

to prove I can choose any of the futures my family imagined for me.
Of course, I know to trade Spanish for English is to trade one weapon
for another. Of course, I am grateful I have a voice at all. What a gift

it is to dictate how I am remembered. & yet, when I say my name
for all it has inherited, my lungs fill with soot. I inhale
& am cooked alive by light. If I am anything, I am the afterglow
of ash that refuses to remain ash. A child kneeling before an altar,

praying for the blood to wash out of his clothes. I wish I knew
the names of each ancestor that burned so I could forget their names
before learning them. I wish knowing was enough. But I'm certain

I'd end up spitting bullets in a muddy river bank. The water,
blushed red & bloated with ragged boots.

Standing at the Mirror, the Author Writes a Poem for Himself in Which the Word *Hate* Is Replaced with the Word *Forgive*

& while I wait for my eyes to relearn open I forgive myself
for the slow rise   the deep ache in the crane of my neck

from bowing down inside myself   I forgive the surrender
the swollen knee   bruise on my rib   the shape & shade

of an August sunrise   I forgive the fence   I could swear
was the horizon   or at least a way out   I forgive myself

for imagining   a way out is a place I could visit   like a corner café
or ex-lover's thigh   I forgive myself for loving

those who have harmed me   for cooking them dinner
& scalding the rice   forgetting to add pepper   or make myself

a plate   I forgive myself for staying   I forgive myself for staying
until I left my skin   another blanket on the bed   until the sound

of a door opening   turned each room into a reason to leave
I counted each second alone as a tiny victory   until I lost count

which is the only victory that matters   please let healing be
not a season   but the body that still belongs to me   & every day

I remember to buy bread   to hide the keys   beneath the window
succulent or walk along the road   dreaming of anything

other than traffic   is a day I get closer to a future made better
by how I live through it   I forgive myself for failing

today   for falling back into bed & drawing the blinds
give me time   I'll get up I promise   I know it doesn't matter

where I go   every direction is forward   I just have to get there
I take a step   & step naked into the shower   the water

so cold I forget to breathe   my body begs to follow the pearls
falling through the metal grate   to become not quite a ghost

but a shadow just out of frame   I say no   I forgive
I forgive myself   with my body right in front of me

How to Write Heisenberg's Uncertainty Principle into a Promise to Return Home

The further you drive north from the San Diego border
    the more the desert simmers in your throat;
rock & ember cool to ice, coyotes lie coiled beneath barbwire
    with mud matted in their fur.

The further you drive east from your abuelo's gravestone
    the more the light refracts
off its epitaph. Keep driving—until all you remember are gems
    cut against rattlesnake fangs

& how the diamondback evolved muscles strong enough
    to swallow whole rats & rabbits
& a child's fingers. & that kind of power cuts deeper
    than any summer heat

even when California hasn't rained anything but dust
    & singed wheat in years.
The further you travel from a familiar ocean, the more
    you realize you've been hurtling towards

the same water this whole time. It's all a trick of language.
    Anything can be a field
if you walk through it. Anywhere can become you
    once you forget how you got there.

The further you walk across New England, from rose garden
    to snowlit harbor, the colder
your father's voice becomes—a gentle & fading echo
    in the windchill along the Charles River—

it shouts *Brandon* into the water & then freezes over.
    & all you want is to live a life
that makes your father mistake his hands for emeralds.
    He carried you across Los Angeles

to give you the type of home songs are written about.
    & the further you flee from his arms
the more you forget what empires he's toppled & turned
    pathway. What ghosts he's given shelter.

Now when you see sand you think: dead language.
    Dead coyotes. Dead embers.
If you return (when you return) tell him how you stood
    knee deep in Boston winter

& the snow peeled its skin from your feet. Salt rose
    from gravel until verbena flowers
bloomed like busted lips. You brought the desert with you
    & you can't shake it

no matter where you go.

EVENTIDE INTERRUPTED BY PHLEBOTOMY & A COYOTE'S HOWL

My mother taught me to walk
with my arms bent forward
so I am always reaching into the future

& ready to carry anyone who can't
make the journey alone. One night, a coyote
broke into our backyard & slaughtered

both our rabbits. The youngest one survived
till morning, long enough to die cradled
in my mother's arms. A kinder world

to exit than jaws of unrelenting hunger.
My mother just kept shouting, *we can't lose both,*
we can't lose both. The tremor

in her voice, a child frantically collecting
fur hoping to piece the animal back together.
My mother can keep anyone from falling apart

except herself. My whole life I've watched her leave
in pieces: doctors examine tubes of plasma
before removing ligaments, cartilage. Iron

is pumped from her arms, small caravans
of hemoglobin. One day, I'll wake up
& she'll be missing. Don't worry: I'll find her

sitting at the bottom of the stairs,
an impossible mountain. I'll remember my lessons,
how to walk, lift, carry. All I've ever wanted

is to live long enough to help my mother rest,
to give her hilltop & hallelujah. Sweet hallowed earth
where she can sleep, unencumbered by the bodies

she can no longer hold close. Though I fear
she will still be haunted by coyotes howling
in the distance, her joints gnawing

for escape. Even now, her bones whittle down
to lit candle wicks. Even now, she continues
to peel flame from her nightgown & place it softly

back in the hearth. When it finally comes time
for her to leave, will her grief be a garden
or garment she can't unwear? What light

will she head toward? It's strange,
no matter how I write it, the story
always ends the same:

warm mountain air, a mother
sitting by moonlight
as a single rabbit grazes in the meadow.

UNIVERSE ENDING (IN GRATITUDE)

the best way to unbury yourself
is to become a seed & then

something more.
at the family reunion, my father

tells the same old jokes,
but they'll never fail

to break me open, a piñata
of eggshell & precious stones.

do you know a more miraculous joy
than joy that refuses the passage of time,

that pauses wind inside the lung?
everything I love about this world

can pass between my father's front teeth
like a single humming guitar string.

what myth doesn't have a man
cursing god for what is absent

in him? after all rage sings
the loudest. but in the short time

I have on this earth—between
the steam engine & last glacial melt—

I choose gratitude.
I choose garden & gravel.

if life is the slow burn of loss
then forgive me

for keeping a few extra matches
in my pocket. for collecting atlases

& shoveling ash into my stomach.
more than anything I am afraid of forgetting

where I came from. what if tomorrow
I turn around & can't place all the people

smiling. or worse
what if all I see is a string of skulls

held together by fishing line, the hook
in my lip. if memory is a bridge

built with marbled brick
then do not worry whether it's safe

to cross. come. let's sit against the ledge
knowing we won't jump. dangle our feet

while we take turns guessing
where the bridge might end: pasture.

padlocked room. well that spits out
maracas ornamented with opal.

if I must fail to outlive myself,
know I am still thankful

we met here today.
grateful neither of us vanished

before we found the other.
the best way to unend yourself

is to build a door in the dark,
people will come for miles

to find it. can you believe
I have a name. I have a name

that someone—who had not yet
met me—wrote down in ink

& wondered what it might sound like
swaddled in skin.

NOTES

"dry/spell" could not exist without the guidance of José Carlos Zepeda Baca.

"In the Story, the Role of Ahab Is Played by My Father" is after Jason Bayani.

"In Defense of Hella" is for April Wildes.

"serpent crown lined with marrow" & "Field Notes on Desire" are in conversation with poems by Jess Rizkallah.

"Etymology of Absence, Ending in a Still Life of the Rio Grande at Sunset" was drafted using a collaboration poem originally written with Porsha Olayiwola.

"Standing at the Mirror, the Author Writes a Poem for Himself in Which the Word *Hate* Is Replaced with the Word *Forgive*" is for Brad Trumpfheller.

"Universe Ending (in Gratitude)" is for my father.

ACKNOWLEDGMENTS

Endless appreciation to the following publications for believing in these poems enough to give them loving first homes. The poems were sometimes published in earlier forms & under different names:

Academy of American Poets: "serpent crown lined with marrow"

The Adroit Journal: "I Watch the Family Move into the House at the End of the Block," "Reino, or I See My Grandfather by the Side of the Road, about Where He's Buried, but He's Wandering around with a Flag of Vertebrae," "Taphephobia, the Morning after I Learn Chester Bennington Took His Own Life"

Anomaly: "Field Notes on Desire," "The First Time I See My Father Cry He Is Pulling Me from the Water to Unsing Alcoholism," "How to Write Heisenberg's Uncertainty Principle into a Promise to Return Home"

Black Warrior Review: "serpent crown lined with marrow"

The Boiler: "line/age," "Conjuring"

decomP magazinE: "Glass Pulled from the Wreckage Like a Body Still Breathing"

diode: "Lupus," "Taphephobia, the Morning after I Learn Chester Bennington Took His Own Life"

Duende: "Desmadre," "dry/spell"

F(r)iction: "Los Fantasmas, or If You've Seen *Coco* You'll Understand Why I Didn't Stop Crying for a Week After"

Frontier: "Standing at the Mirror, the Author Writes a Poem for Himself in Which the Word *Hate* Is Replaced with the Word *Forgive*"

Glass: A Journal of Poetry: "Universe Ending (in Gratitude)"

Hobart: "Raw, or My Therapist Asks Me to Describe the Feeling without Using 'I' Statements," "origin :: predisposition," "portrait of anxiety as liminal space," "The Author Becomes a Moirologist"

The Journal: "Blood Pageantry"

Lunch Ticket: "American Boy Shares Death Metal with His Abuelo"

the minnesota review: "That Time I Went North & Woke Up with a New Face"

Muzzle Magazine: "I Feel Most Like Myself with Painted Nails"

Ninth Letter: "Etymology of Absence, Ending in My Grandmother Singing 'México en la Piel'"

PANK: "Etymology of Absence, Ending in a Still Life of the Rio Grande at Sunset"

Poetry Daily: "serpent crown lined with marrow"

Rust + Moth: "Portrait of Grief as a Manicured Lawn"

The Shallow Ends: "As Respite from Insomnia, the Author Writes an Elegy for What the Night Took"

Shenandoah: "Ethos Of ICE," "Eventide Interrupted by Phlebotomy & a Coyote's Howl"

Sixth Finch: "In Defense of Hella"

Split Lip Magazine: "Alprazolam"

Tinderbox Poetry Journal: "Reino, or I See My Grandfather by the Side of the Road, about Where He's Buried, but He's Wandering around with a Flag of Vertebrae," "Synonyms for Border," "Architecture of Refuge"

Up the Staircase: "Theorem with Staircase & Hummingbird," "Every Time I See My Ex, Shit Gets Kafkaesque" "serpent crown lined with marrow" was republished with the *Academy of American Poets* as part of the 2018 Academy of American Poets Prize.

"Reino, or I See My Grandfather by the Side of the Road, about Where He's Buried, but He's Wandering around with a Flag of Vertebrae" & "Taphephobia, the Morning after I Learn Chester Bennington Took His Own Life" were republished by *The Adroit Journal* as part of the 2018 Gregory Djanikian Scholarship.

"Los Fantasmas, or If You've Seen *Coco* You'll Understand Why I Didn't Stop Crying for a Week After" was a finalist for the fall 2017 *F(r)iction* poetry contest.

I am humbled by all the people who helped this book become a reality. I do not deserve you. Gratitude to the 2018 House Slam Team: Porsha Olayiwola, Golden, Julissa "Juju" Emile, Anita D. Thank you to Jess Rizkallah, & Brad Trumpfheller for teaching me what poems can do. I love you. Thank you to the CalSLAM family who raised me: Gabriel Cortez, Natasha Huey, Jade Cho, Isa Borgeson, Terry Taplin, Jonathan Pyner, Leslie Valencia, Brandon Young & Victoria Massie. Thank you to John Skoyles & Aya de Leon for your mentorship. To Hanif Abdurraqib, Porsha Olayiwola, & George Abraham, gratitude for your kind words & your brilliance. To Ben Grenrock & Dave "Bones McQueen" Lee, you two are geniuses. I adore you both so much.

To all the people who have mentored me, shared space with me, & allowed me to love them as fiercely as I do, thank you: Allison Truj, Myles Taylor, Tim "Toaster" Henderson, Lip Manegio, Jaime Zuckerman, Evan Cutts, Mckendy Fils-Aimé, Neiel Israel, Simone Beaubien, Zeke Russell, Jaz Sufi, Jason Bayani, Jordan Ranft, Brennan DeFrisco, Imani Cezanne, Arman Sufi, José Carlos Zepeda Baca, James Merenda, Kofi Dadzie, Oompa, Abe Becker, Dana Alsamsam, April Wildes, Reid Latimer, John Taylor, Rikki Angelides, Sean Dever, Duke Trott, Anna Binkowitz, Rebecca Lynn, Kayla LaRosa, Sara Mae, Dessaline Etienne, Holden Bender-Bernstein, Joshua Merchant, Michelle Jackson, Brian Hamilton, John Pinkham, Victoria Morgan, Kevan Mai, Nghiem Le, Melissa Rogers Hamady, Justin Hamady, Antonio Appling, Timothy "Big Brother" Cheung,

Michelle Betters, Holly Wilson, Jazzy Dena, Lindsey Williams, Zenaida Peterson, Cassandra de Alba, Sally Burnette, Nora Meiners, JR Mahung, Marlena Reimer, Jenny Heath, Chestina Craig, Sheila Sadr, Mark Maza, Angelica Aguilera, Asia Bryant-Wilkerson, Aleah Bradshaw, Sam Rush, CJ West, Katie Edwards, Robbie Dunning, Sarah Perry, Will Giles, Nazelah Jamison, Betsy Gomez, Kay Nilsson, Adrianne Smith, Skylar Kergil, Simone Cardona, Naomi Hester, Miguel Mendoza, Meghan Camacho, Samantha Parks, Matteo Porcedda, Abigael Cho, Alicia Armijo, Robert Malloy, Victoria Passiflora, Kieran Collier, Kareem Asha, Sophia Holtz, Chloé Cunha.

Gratitude to Derrick C. Brown, Lino Anunciacion, & the whole Write Bloody family for seeing my vision & allowing me the space to write, & to David Perez & Gary Edwin Lovely for your keen insight.

Gratitude to the MFA program at Emerson College & the Poetry for the People program at UC Berkeley for nurturing me.

Thank you to my parents for challenging me to live compassionately, & to my brothers, Joshua & Kyle, for putting up with me. To all my familia, blood & otherwise, I write for you.

Lastly, thank you, dear reader. I am grateful to share this world with you.

I've been here for too long to face this on my own.
Well, I guess this is growing up.
—Mark Hoppus

ABOUT THE AUTHOR

BRANDON MELENDEZ is a Mexican-American poet from California and a graduate from UC Berkeley. A recipient of the 2018 Djanikian Scholarship from *The Adroit Journal*, and the 2018 Academy of American Poets Award, he was also awarded "Best Poem" and "Funniest Poem" at the College Unions Poetry Slam Invitational (CUPSI). His poems can be found in *Black Warrior Review*, *Muzzle Magazine*, *Ninth Letter*, *PANK*, *Shenandoah*, and elsewhere. He is currently an MFA candidate at Emerson College.

www.brandonmelendezpoet.com

IF YOU LIKE BRANDON MELENDEZ, BRANDON LIKES...

Amulet
Jason Bayani

Pecking Order
Nicole Homer

This Way to the Sugar
Hieu Minh Nguyen

Floating, Brilliant, Gone
Franny Choi

Favorite Daughter
Nancy Huang

Write Bloody Publishing publishes and promotes great books of poetry every year. We believe that poetry can change the world for the better. We are an independent press dedicated to quality literature and book design, with an office in Los Angeles, California.

We are grassroots, DIY, bootstrap believers. Pull up a good book and join the family. Support independent authors, artists, and presses.

Want to know more about Write Bloody books, authors, and events? Join our mailing list at

www.writebloody.com

Write Bloody Books

CPSIA information can be obtained
at www.ICGtesting.com
Printed in the USA
FSHW020136060319